FOOD SCIENTISTS IN ACTION

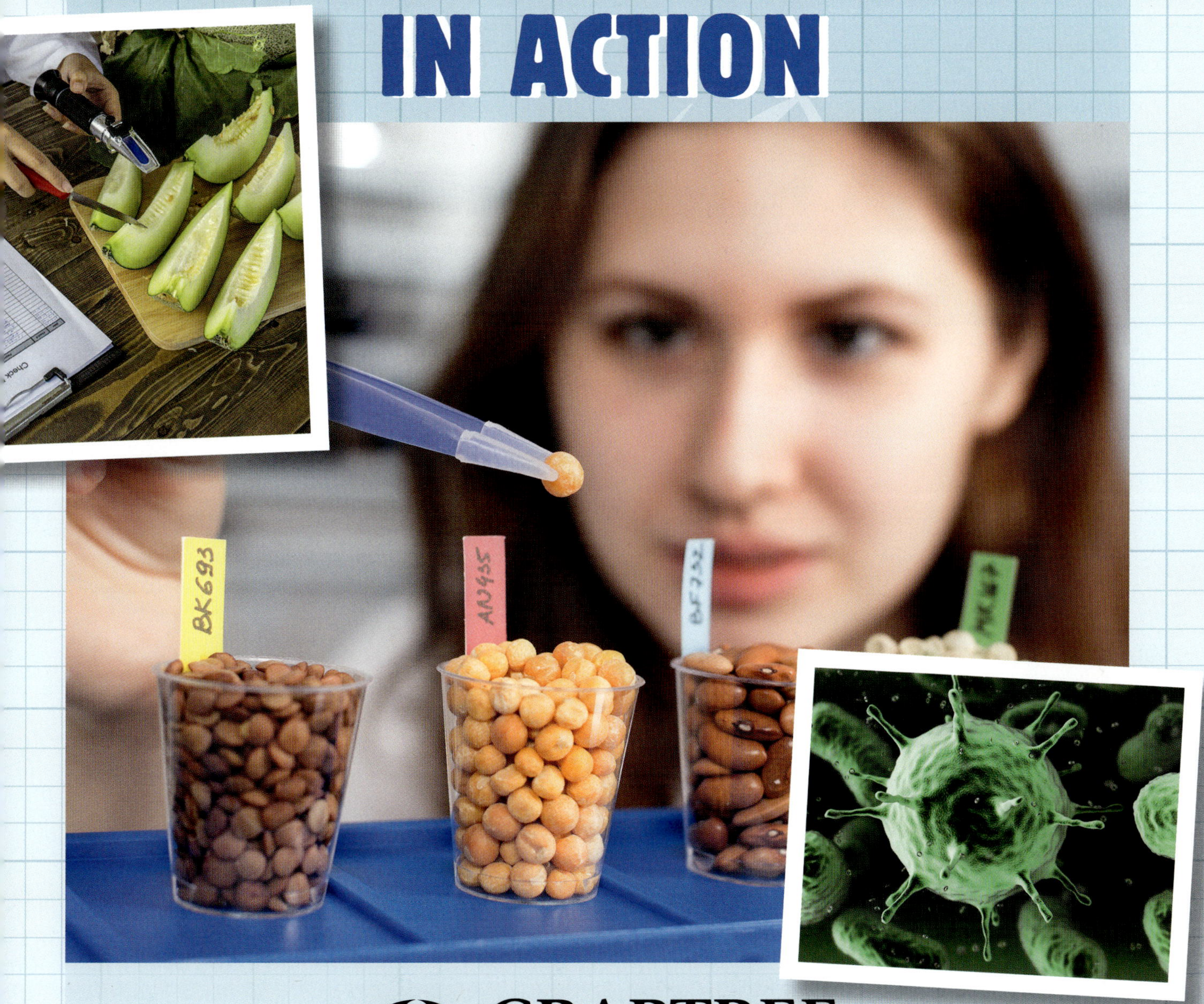

Robin Johnson

Author: Robin Johnson

Series research and development: Reagan Miller

Editorial director: Kathy Middleton

Photo research: James Nixon, Robin Johnson

Editors: Paul Humphrey, James Nixon, Ellen Rodger

Proofreader: Lorna Notsch

Designer: Keith Williams (sprout.uk.com)

Prepress technician: Samara Parent

Print coordinator: Katherine Berti

Illustrator: Keith Williams (sprout.uk.com)

Consultant: Brianne Manning

Produced for Crabtree Publishing Company by Discovery Books

Cover image: A food scientist analyzes a tomato in a laboratory

Photographs:

Alamy: pp. 4 top (dpa picture alliance), 9 bottom (Vaclav Salek/CTK Photo), 15 top (NASA Photo), 17 top (H. Mark Weidman Photography), 20 (Nature and Science), 21 bottom (dpa picture alliance archive), 23 top (age fotostock), 29 bottom (Marmaduke St. John).
Getty Images: pp. 5 (Akio Kon/Bloomberg), 9 top (Simon Dawson/Bloomberg), 10 (EVARISTO SA/AFP), 11 top (Martin Leissl/Bloomberg), 13 (Corey Lowenstein/Raleigh News & Observer/TNS), 16 bottom (Gary Tramontina/Sygma), 18 (John Tlumacki/The Boston Globe), 24 top (John Smierciak/Chicago Tribune/MCT), 28 bottom (Simon Dawson/Bloomberg), 29 top (Deon Raath/Foto24/Gallo Images).
McMaster University: p. 22.
NASA: p. 19 top.
Shutterstock: pp. 4 bottom (CatherineL-Prod), 6 top (Chromatika Multimedia), 6 bottom (Lordn), 7 top (Vlad Teodor), 7 bottom (Suwin), 8 top (Everett Collection), 11 bottom (thodonal88), 14 (science photo), 15 bottom (AR Images), 16 top (Supavadee butradee), 19 bottom (Linnas), 21 top (Evgeniy Kalinovskiy), 23 bottom (baibaz), 24 bottom (Robyn Mackenzie), 25 top (Suzanne Tucker), 25 bottom (Charles Knowles), 28 top (Tinxi).
Wikimedia: pp. 8 bottom, 12 (NASA), 17 bottom (NASA).
All other images from Shutterstock

Library and Archives Canada Cataloguing in Publication

Johnson, Robin (Robin R.), author
Food scientists in action / Robin Johnson.

(Scientists in action)
Includes index.
Issued in print and electronic formats.
ISBN 978-0-7787-5207-3 (hardcover).--
ISBN 978-0-7787-5218-9 (softcover).--
ISBN 978-1-4271-2159-2 (HTML)

1. Food--Juvenile literature. 2. Food--Analysis--Juvenile literature. 3. Food--Composition--Juvenile literature. 4. Scientists--Juvenile literature. I. Title.

TX355.J647 2018 j641.3 C2018-903006-2
C2018-903007-0

Library of Congress Cataloging-in-Publication Data

Names: Johnson, Robin (Robin R.), author.
Title: Food scientists in action / Robin Johnson.
Description: New York, New York : Crabtree Publishing, [2019] | Series: Scientists in action | Includes index.
Identifiers: LCCN 2018033709 (print) | LCCN 2018034465 (ebook) | ISBN 9781427121592 (Electronic) | ISBN 9780778752073 (hardcover) | ISBN 9780778752189 (pbk.)
Subjects: LCSH: Food--Research--Juvenile literature. | Food industry and trade--Juvenile literature. | Food--Miscellanea--Juvenile literature.
Classification: LCC TX355 (ebook) | LCC TX355 .J65 2019 (print) | DDC 664--dc23
LC record available at https://lccn.loc.gov/2018033709

Crabtree Publishing Company
www.crabtreebooks.com 1-800-387-7650

Printed in the U.S.A./102018/CG20180810

Published in Canada
Crabtree Publishing
616 Welland Ave.
St. Catharines, Ontario
L2M 5V6

Published in the United States
Crabtree Publishing
PMB 59051
350 Fifth Avenue, 59th Floor
New York, New York 10118

Published in the United Kingdom
Crabtree Publishing
Maritime House
Basin Road North, Hove
BN41 1WR

Published in Australia
Crabtree Publishing
3 Charles Street
Coburg North
VIC, 3058

CONTENTS

FOOD FOR THOUGHT

A scientist is experimenting with a tasty new energy bar. It contains bananas, honey, vanilla—and crickets. The scientist has studied these insects as a food source and knows that they are safe to eat. In fact, crickets are packed with **protein** and are a good source of **nutrients**. Scientists are always looking for new ways to feed the world's growing population. They work hard to ensure that everyone has safe, fresh, tasty, and nutritious food to eat. They are food scientists in action!

These scientists are investigating insects as a food source for people.

What Is a Food Scientist?

Food science is the study of the physical and chemical nature of foods and the changes that take place in them. Some changes occur naturally in foods. For example, the bananas in your fruit bowl ripen and spoil naturally over time. Other changes occur when food is processed. To process food means to cook, package, and change fresh foods in other ways into products that people can buy to eat. For example, fresh bananas can be processed into pudding cups or frozen banana cream pies. People who work in this field—known as food scientists—investigate all aspects of food and food processing.

This energy bar is made from crickets and other insects. Crickets have a nutty taste and are good for you.

Finding Solutions

Food science is an applied science. That means that food scientists use science and engineering knowledge to answer questions and find solutions to problems. They carry out complex research to understand and improve our food supply. For example, some scientists try to make food products more nutritious. They might investigate ways to fortify foods, which means adding **vitamins** and **minerals** to them. Other food scientists improve how food is produced, packaged, or stored. They might develop new materials that increase the **shelf life** of packaged foods.

In this book, we will look at how these scientists study food, the questions they've answered, and the problems they are still trying to solve. We will also examine how food scientists use science practices to guide their investigations and make discoveries in their field.

The Science of Food

Some food scientists work in kitchens, but they are not chefs! Chefs combine food ingredients to make tasty new recipes. Food scientists develop new products by analyzing the chemicals in food and how they react in different ways.

This food scientist is studying a single-celled organism called euglena. Scientists in Japan are using this organism to make smoothies and other food items.

ON THE JOB

Food safety and healthy eating are major concerns for food scientists. They carefully analyze food to ensure that it does not contain harmful bacteria. Bacteria are tiny organisms that can only be seen with a microscope. Some bacteria can make people sick. Scientists add ingredients and design packaging that help prevent harmful bacteria from forming or growing in food. They also try to keep helpful bacteria from being destroyed when food is processed. For example, the bacteria in some yogurts may help people **digest** food.

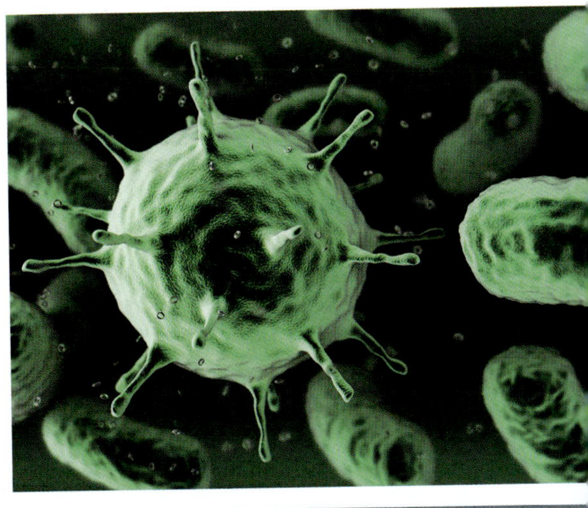

Some food scientists analyze tiny bacteria like these under microscopes.

Every Step of the Way

Food scientists are on the job at every step of the production process. Their work begins after food has been grown and harvested for human use. Some food scientists analyze these **raw ingredients** to make sure that they are safe and ready to be processed. Other food scientists try to improve food products by making them tastier or more nutritious. They might work to reduce the amount of sugar, salt, or fat in foods. Still other food scientists develop and test new foods. If you've ever eaten turducken (roast turkey stuffed with duck that is stuffed with chicken), you can thank a food scientist!

This scientist is analyzing apples to make sure that they are safe to use in food products.

Growing Solutions

Some food scientists also study agricultural science. Scientists in this field might try to grow **sustainable** food crops. They also might modify crops to help them resist pests and disease.

Fields of Study

Food scientists use their knowledge and skills to investigate food in different ways. Some of the main fields of food science are:

Food Chemistry

Food chemists study the chemical processes and changes that take place in food, particularly when it is processed. They experiment with the content, color, flavor, and other qualities of food.

Food Microbiology

Food microbiologists study bacteria and other tiny organisms that live in or create food. They research ways to store food and keep it from spoiling.

Food Engineering

Food engineers develop products and processes to safely handle, package, distribute, and store foods.

Nutrition

Nutrition scientists study health issues surrounding food. They analyze how vitamins, minerals, and other nutrients affect our bodies.

Sensory Science

Sensory scientists study how different foods appeal to the five senses. They conduct research to help food companies develop products that people will like and buy.

This food engineer is inspecting equipment used to bottle beverages in a factory.

THE GROWTH OF FOOD SCIENCE

People have always needed to eat—and have always looked for ways to improve their food. Early people experimented with the products that they hunted and harvested. They used spices for flavor and developed methods to preserve their foods, or keep them from spoiling. For example, people smoked, dried, and salted their meat and fish to make them last longer. People preserved food so that they could survive during the cold winter months when there were few animals to hunt and crops did not grow.

Refrigerators were cool inventions that changed the types of food that people could store and eat.

Nicolas Appert changed the way we can eat foods today.

Fathers of Food Science

In 1795, a French chef named Nicolas Appert began experimenting with ways to preserve soups, juices, jellies, and other foods. He placed the food in thick glass jars, sealed the jars with cork and wax, and then put them in boiling water. Soon foods of all kinds were being manufactured in factories and sold in canning jars. People were still getting sick from bacteria in milk and other beverages, however. In 1864, a French scientist named Louis Pasteur invented a process in which bacteria are destroyed by heating and then cooling liquids. His invention—which is now called pasteurization—helped prevent many serious diseases caused by harmful bacteria.

Food Science Today

Food scientists have changed the way that people **consume** food. Today, there is a greater variety of foods available than ever before. Food stays fresh longer and is more convenient to buy. But there is still much work to be done. Food scientists continue to ask questions and try to solve problems, such as food security. Food security means that all people have access to enough safe and nutritious food to meet their needs at all times. Scientists search for new food sources for people and animals. They look for **environmentally friendly** ways to manufacture food and reduce waste. They continue to improve the taste, variety, and nutritional content of foods. And they are always looking for the next great flavor or food innovation.

A food scientist experiments with dried peppers as a new snack food.

Processed foods, such as potato chips, are produced in factories.

Processed Food

Processed food makes up about 60 percent of the American diet today. Processed food includes breakfast cereal, packaged snacks, lunch meat, chicken nuggets, frozen pizzas, and instant soups. These foods are convenient but often contain **artificial** sweeteners, flavors, and dyes that may be harmful to the human body. Some food scientists are investigating natural substances that could replace these chemicals in processed foods.

INVESTIGATING LIFE

All scientists ask questions about the world around them. They conduct research and search for evidence to support their answers. They use science practices (see box) to gather information, repeating some or all of the steps as needed. These science practices describe the methods that scientists use to investigate **phenomena** and **formulate** theories about the natural world.

Science Practices

The science practices are:

- Asking questions
- Developing and using models
- Planning and carrying out investigations
- Analyzing and interpreting **data**
- Using mathematics and **computational thinking**
- Constructing explanations
- Engaging in arguments from evidence
- Obtaining, evaluating, and communicating information

Observation and Experiments

Scientists in different fields investigate in different ways. Some scientists use observation to gather evidence. Observation is the process of using scientific equipment to obtain and record data. The scientists analyze and interpret, or make sense of, the data they have collected. Other scientists plan and carry out experiments. They might develop and use models to display the results of their experiments. Models are objects or images that are used to show or explain ideas. Scientists might use mathematics and computational thinking to make sense of their findings and construct explanations. Then they formulate arguments from the evidence they have gathered and communicate that information.

This food scientist is preparing vegetable samples for observation in a lab.

Investigating Food

In their quest for answers to their questions, food scientists use both observation and experiments. They collect food samples and carefully observe them in laboratories. Scientists might observe foods to see if they lose nutrients when they are frozen. They might make observations about enzymes in food. Enzymes are chemical substances in animals and plants that help digestion and other natural processes occur. Food scientists also plan and carry out experiments in labs and **test kitchens**. For example, they might experiment with natural substances to replace artificial food additives. Additives are chemical substances that are added to food products to make them last longer or to improve their flavor, appearance, or other qualities.

This food scientist has a sweet job! She is experimenting with candy samples in a test kitchen.

Food scientists are experimenting with ways to make chopping onions less tearful.

No More Tears

Do you cry when you chop onions? Food scientists in Japan are cooking up a solution for that! They discovered an enzyme in onions that produces a chemical that stings our eyes. The chemical is released from onions when they are cut, and our eyes water to flush it out. Now the food scientists are developing onions without the tear-jerking enzyme.

HUNGRY FOR ANSWERS

Food scientists question everything about food. Some food scientists ask questions about food itself. They ask how ingredients can be changed to improve the quality or taste of foods. They ask how food products can be made totally safe for everyone to eat. For example, some food scientists analyze food products to make sure they do not contain common allergens, such as peanuts, tree nuts, wheat, and eggs. Allergens are substances that cause allergic reactions.

Out of This World

Food scientists ask questions about food all around the world. Some even ask questions about food that is out of this world! Food scientists who work for NASA (the National Aeronautics and Space Administration) and other space agencies develop food for astronauts. These scientists investigate ways to improve the taste and variety of space foods. They search for new foods for astronauts to eat and new methods to feed them. They ask how crews can access clean drinking water. And they ask how foods can be preserved for longer and longer periods of time. Today, the average space mission takes six months to complete. But astronauts are preparing for missions to Mars that could last as long as five years!

Developing safe, tasty, and nutritious food for astronauts is the mission of NASA's food scientists.

Can It Be Harmful?

Other food scientists ask what effects freezing, heating, drying, canning, and other processes have on food. For example, food scientists are studying a chemical called Bisphenol A (BPA) that is often used to coat the inside of metal food cans. The chemical helps to preserve the food. However, scientists have discovered that BPA seeps into some canned foods—such as soups and pastas—more than others, which could lead to health problems. They are investigating the canning process and the possible effects of this chemical on people who consume it.

From the Field: John Sheppard

Can wild **yeasts** be used to make beer and other food products? That was the question that inspired process engineer John Sheppard. Sheppard studies fermentation and other biological processes at North Carolina State University. Fermentation is the process by which yeast converts sugar into alcohol. Yeasts are usually grown in large tanks for use in the food industry, but they are also found in nature. Sheppard investigated the wild yeasts found on wasps and bees. He experimented with the yeasts and collected data about how they grew. He discovered that by making small changes to the fermentation process, the same yeast species created beer with very different flavors, such as honey and apple. Sheppard's findings could be applied to other foods that contain yeast, such as bread, pickles, yogurt, and cheese.

John Sheppard (right) investigates the fermentation process in his university lab.

INVESTIGATING FOOD

Scientists investigate food to answer questions and find solutions to problems. They make detailed observations about food and food processes. They analyze the appearance, color, texture, odor, **consistency**, and other physical properties of food. Physical properties can be observed and measured without changing the food itself. Food scientists also observe the chemical changes that take place in food when it is frozen, heated, or treated in other ways.

This researcher is analyzing food samples in a lab—and being careful not to spill the beans!

Ground Control

Most food scientists plan and carry out their research in labs or test kitchens. Some visit factories to develop machinery or inspect finished food products. NASA food scientists also conduct research in space! For example, scientists sent kits containing tortillas, salmon, and other foods to the **International Space Station**. They kept the kits in orbit for varying amounts of time and then brought them back down to Earth. The scientists compared the food items to identical kits that did not go into space and made observations about them. Today, food scientists are preparing for missions to Mars and investigating how higher levels of **radiation** in deep space could affect food.

Houston, We Have a Problem

Scientists who investigate food for space missions have many factors to consider. First of all, the **gravity** in space is very weak. That means that astronauts and their tuna sandwiches float all around. Food must be sticky or wet so it does not create crumbs that could damage valuable equipment. There are no refrigerators or freezers in space (they use up too much energy), so food must be stored at room temperature for long periods of time. Food must be compact, lightweight, and nutritious. And it must be familiar and tasty so that astronauts will eat enough to get the nutrients that they need.

Tortillas are ideal for space missions because they do not create crumbs.

Down-to-Earth Problem

Gravity can be a problem on Earth, too—especially when it causes your ice cream to drip down to the ground! Scientists in Colombia and Canada are working together to solve that problem. They cannot change the force of gravity, but they can change how fast ice cream melts. The scientists found that adding tiny, flavorless **fibers** from banana stalks (left over after the bananas have been picked) causes ice cream to melt at a much slower rate.

TOOLS OF THE TRADE

Food scientists use a variety of equipment to investigate food. The types of tools they use depend on their role in the food industry. For example, some food scientists use refractometers to measure the sugar in foods and salt analyzers to study their salt content. Other food scientists use devices called consistometers to check the consistency of sauces and salad dressings. There are even tools—called colorimeters and olfactometers—that measure the color and smell of foods!

This food scientist is using a refractometer to measure the sugar content of melons.

Green Ketchup

Color plays an important role in our sense of taste. If we think that food is the wrong color, our brains will tell us that it does not taste good. Food scientists at Heinz learned that lesson the hard way. In 2000, they developed a new green ketchup. It was a hit with monster-loving kids but few others, and the company soon stopped producing it.

The Metric System

All food scientists use the metric system to measure and record their findings. Using one system of measurement allows scientists around the world to understand, compare, and share data.

Quality Control

Some food scientists use tools to test and inspect food products before people consume them. They check the food to make sure that it meets certain standards. A standard is a level of quality that is considered acceptable. Food companies set standards for their products. Governments also make rules and regulations about food and how it is made to keep the public safe. Food scientists use tools to help enforce these rules. For example, they might use **pH** meters to test the **acidity** of milk. The normal pH value of milk is about 6.7. When milk goes sour, it becomes more acidic and its pH value is lower.

This food scientist has a lot of work to ketchup on! She is testing ketchup to make sure that it is good to eat.

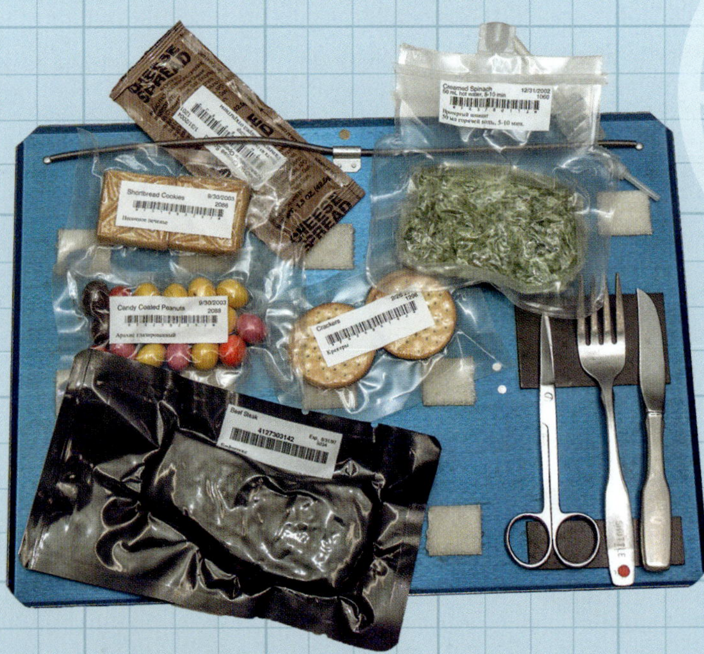

A variety of freeze-dried foods have been developed for astronauts to eat in space.

Space Kitchens

Scientists who develop space food use equipment that other food scientists will not use on a regular basis. They use freeze dryers to remove the water from foods, such as soup and scrambled eggs. Removing water from food makes it lighter and more compact to send into space. Astronauts later add water back to the food before eating it. Food scientists also use equipment to irradiate meat, or expose it to radiation. They cook, package, and then irradiate beef, chicken, and other meats to destroy harmful bacteria that could make astronauts sick.

GATHERING DATA

Food scientists gather data from the investigations that they carry out in their labs and test kitchens. Some food scientists also conduct taste tests to collect information from people. A taste test is a form of research in which people are given samples of food to eat or drink. Scientists ask the testers to rate the flavor, texture, color, and other aspects of the food. They conduct detailed **surveys** and record what the testers did or did not like about the samples. Some food scientists also gather data by tasting food themselves. They might test new foods that they are developing or check finished products to ensure that they meet certain standards.

From the Field: Hélène Marsot

Hélène Marsot wakes up and smells the coffee. As a food scientist for an international company, her job is to ensure that millions of cups of coffee served around the world all taste exactly the same. Marsot—who holds master's degrees in food microbiology and sensory evaluation—developed a system for scoring the coffee that she samples. She rates each cup on its aroma, sweetness, acidity, fragrance, balance, body, and finish. If one cup fails even one of the seven criteria, the entire shipment of coffee may be rejected.

Hélène Marsot drinks as many as 100 cups of coffee a day in the name of science.

Using the Data

Once food scientists have collected and recorded data, they return to their labs or offices. They put all the information together and try to interpret their findings. Some food scientists develop graphs, models, and other visual aids to display their data. For example, they might develop **molecular** models to show the chemical changes that take place in foods. Molecular models are objects that show atoms (the smallest parts of matter), the bonds that hold them together, and their processes.

It is crucial that astronauts taste-test their meals before going into space. If they don't like their food, they may not eat enough to get the nutrients that they need to stay healthy.

Lost in Space

Food scientists at NASA recently gathered data about how time affects the nutrients in space food. They measured 24 vitamins and minerals in more than 100 foods that were freeze-dried, irradiated, and processed for space in other ways. They stored the foods at room temperature for a period of three years. At the end of the study, the scientists compiled their data and displayed the results in a series of graphs. Their evidence showed that foods lost large amounts of vitamins B_1 and C over time. Now the scientists are investigating ways to fortify space foods or process them in new ways so that they keep these and other vitamins for longer periods of time.

This molecular model shows the structure of vitamin C.

SHARING FOOD SCIENCE

After food scientists have finished their investigations, they communicate their results. They tell fellow scientists and the public what they have discovered about food and food processes. It is important for food scientists to share their research so that people can make informed choices about the foods that they eat. Sharing investigations with the scientific community also allows scientists to learn from each other and build on that knowledge. It can spark further questions and inspire more investigations—and help scientists find solutions to food problems.

These food scientists are sharing the results of a study about sodium. Sodium is a soft, white chemical element that combines with other chemicals in nature to form salt.

The Proof Is in the Paper

Food scientists write reports that clearly and carefully explain all aspects of their research. The reports outline the questions that the scientists asked, the methods and materials that they used, and the data that they gathered. The papers also outline the results that the scientists achieved and the conclusions that they reached. For example, NASA scientists reported the results of their space radiation experiment (see page 14). They concluded that the foods sent into orbit lost nutrients at about the same rate as identical foods that stayed on Earth.

From the Field: Jane K. Parker

Jane K. Parker thought outside the kitchen—and built on the work of scientists in another field. Parker is a British chemist whose research focuses on food flavors and how different chemical reactions create them. She recently carried out an investigation to make smoked foods safer to eat. Meat, fish, and other foods are sometimes treated with smoke to give them a woodsy flavor. But smoking foods can create low levels of carcinogens—substances that could cause cancer. Parker read a science paper about the filters used in car tailpipes to reduce harmful **emissions**—and it sparked an idea. She experimented and discovered that the same type of material could also be used to filter smoke for foods.

These sausages have been produced and smoked at a meat processing plant.

Not-So-Secret Recipes

Some food scientists publish their research in books or **scientific journals**. For example, NASA food scientists published the results of their space radiation experiment in the *Journal of Food Science*. Other food scientists write articles or give interviews for newspapers, magazines, or websites. Still other food scientists present their work at public science meetings called conferences. Researchers from around the world gather at conferences to discuss their work and find out what's cooking in the field of food science.

This food scientist is sharing her research at a conference in Germany. She is investigating insects as a food source for astronauts.

COOKING UP SOLUTIONS

Have you ever heard someone say that there are too many cooks in the kitchen? That means that too many people are working on something all at once. When it comes to test kitchens for food science, that saying does not apply! In fact, it is helpful to have different tools, skills, knowledge, and points of view at the table. Food scientists often collaborate, or work together, to share information. Collaboration allows food scientists to connect with other scientists who are carrying out similar research or searching for solutions to the same types of problems.

The Solution Is Clear

About 600 million people get sick from **contaminated** food each year. Researchers at McMaster University in Canada are working together to solve that problem. Biochemists and engineers at the school collaborated to design a small, clear patch that detects harmful bacteria in meat, milk, and other foods. The patch—which is dotted with tiny drops of harmless **DNA** molecules—could be incorporated into food packaging so that it touches the product inside. People could use their smartphones to scan the patch, which lights up if food is contaminated—a bright idea for food safety.

Researchers at McMaster University examine the little patch that could have a huge impact on food safety.

Comparing Results

Food scientists also share their findings so that other scientists can corroborate them. To corroborate something means to support it with evidence. Food scientists compare their findings with the work of other scientists in their field. If the scientists have carried out similar investigations and achieved similar results, their conclusions are probably accurate.

Food Reviews

Food studies must undergo peer review, which means that they are thoroughly checked by other scientific experts in the same field. This is particularly important in the field of food science, in which one mistake could be a matter of life or death. The scientists carefully examine all aspects of the research to check for any errors or bias that may have occurred. Bias takes place when the results of a study are influenced in some way. For example, food scientists often conduct blind taste tests, which means that testers do not know the brand or type of food that they are trying. This helps eliminate bias, because the testers might rate a food item based on the brand instead of how it tastes.

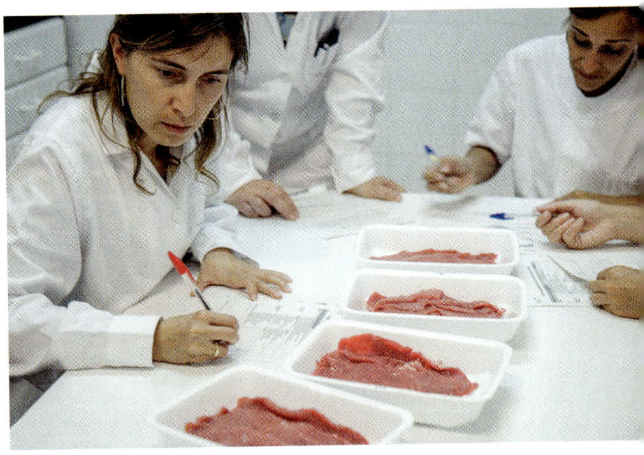

Food investigations must be thoroughly checked before they are published in scientific journals.

Some people believe that goji berries, chia seeds, and other foods have the power to fight cancer and other diseases. But many scientists warn that these and other "superfoods" could cause more health problems than they solve.

Fake Food News

If a research study is flawed or inaccurate, it will not be accepted by the scientific community. The study could still make its way into the news or online, however. That is why it is important to check facts before you believe myths about the food that you eat.

INVESTIGATE!

Get a taste of food science with this hands-on cereal experiment! It has you asking questions about the foods that you eat each day. It will show you how to plan and carry out an investigation and then analyze and interpret the data that you collect. You will learn how to obtain information and use it to construct an explanation. And you will find out which cereals make the breakfast of champions!

This food scientist is mixing cereal ingredients in a large tool called a V-blender.

Iron Concentration

Scientists often experiment with additives in breakfast cereals and other processed foods. They might add substances to make foods taste sweeter, look more colorful, or stay fresh longer. They also add vitamins and minerals to processed foods to make them more nutritious. For example, food scientists often add iron to cereals. Iron is a metal that is found all over Earth. It is also a nutrient that people need to stay healthy. Iron helps our blood carry oxygen to all our cells. Without oxygen, our cells can't make enough energy for us to survive. Our bodies cannot produce iron, so we must eat foods that have iron in them. Some foods naturally contain iron, but most breakfast cereals must be fortified to be good sources of iron.

Foods such as beef, liver, eggs, spinach, peas, beans, and raisins are natural sources of iron.

You can carry out experiments on your breakfast cereal.

Materials

- Four boxes of breakfast cereal with different amounts of iron (for example, 15%, 30%, 50%, and 75% Daily Value)
- 68 ounces (2L) of **distilled water**
- Blender
- Four clean, clear, 34-ounce (1L) plastic bottles with smooth sides
- Large bowl
- Large metric measuring cup with a spout
- Another small metric measuring cup
- Heavy-duty magnet
- Scissors
- Duct tape
- Marker
- Notebook or paper

Ask a Question

The first step in scientific investigation is asking questions. Write down some questions that you would like to answer about the iron in breakfast cereal. For example, how much iron is in the cereal that you eat each day? Which cereals have the highest and lowest amounts of iron? Are the **Nutrition Facts** labels on cereal boxes accurate? Then gather the materials from the list (right) and turn to the next page to carry out the investigation.

What can you learn from the Nutrition Facts labels on cereal boxes and other food products?

Daily Value

The Percent Daily Value shows how much one serving of food counts toward the nutrients that you need each day. You will find this information on the Nutrition Facts label on the side of cereal boxes.

TEST YOUR METAL

Follow these steps to complete your cereal experiment.

Procedure

1. Carefully cut the bottom off all four plastic bottles and remove their lids. You will use the bottles as funnels in this experiment.
2. Tape the magnet to the outside of one of the bottles about halfway down. Write the name of the cereal on the bottle.
3. Put 1 cup (250 ml) of one type of cereal into the blender. Add 1 cup (250 ml) of distilled water. Blend the cereal and water until you have a smooth mixture without any lumps. Pour the mixture into the large measuring cup.
4. Pour 1.5 tablespoons (22ml) of distilled water into the blender to rinse it out. Then add the rinse to the cereal mixture.
5. Hold the bottle with the magnet on it above the bowl. Position the bottle on its side so that the magnet is facing down and the wide end of the bottle is slightly higher than the small opening. Slowly pour the cereal mixture through the bottle and into the bowl. Make sure that the magnet stays facedown so that the mixture inside the bottle passes over it.
6. If the mixture is too thick to pour, put it back in the blender. Add 1/2 cup (118ml) of distilled water and blend it again. Then try pouring the mixture through the bottle again. You may need to repeat this step several times.
7. After all the cereal mixture has passed through the bottle, pour another 3/4 cup (177 ml) of distilled water through to rinse out the cereal and clean the iron that is left behind.
8. Empty out any water that is left in the bottle. Then remove the magnet and set the bottle in a safe place to dry. Repeat steps 2 to 8 with the other three cereals.

9 Leave the bottles to dry for one to two hours. Then compare the size of the iron pellets that you collected in each bottle and make a scale to rate them. For example, the value if no iron was collected could be 0. The value of the largest piece of iron could be 10. Give each pellet a number value and record the data on a piece of paper.

NAME OF CEREAL	PERCENT DAILY VALUE OF IRON (%)	DID A PELLET FORM? (Y/N)	RELATIVE IRON PELLET SIZE
Cereal 1	15	Y	4
Cereal 2	30	Y	5
Cereal 3	50	Y	6
Cereal 4	75	Y	9

10 Make a data table to display your results (as shown on the right).

11 Display your data on a graph. Write a scale for the Percent Daily Value of iron on the y-axis and a scale for the relative iron pellet sizes on the x-axis. Draw a circle or other symbol where the values meet.

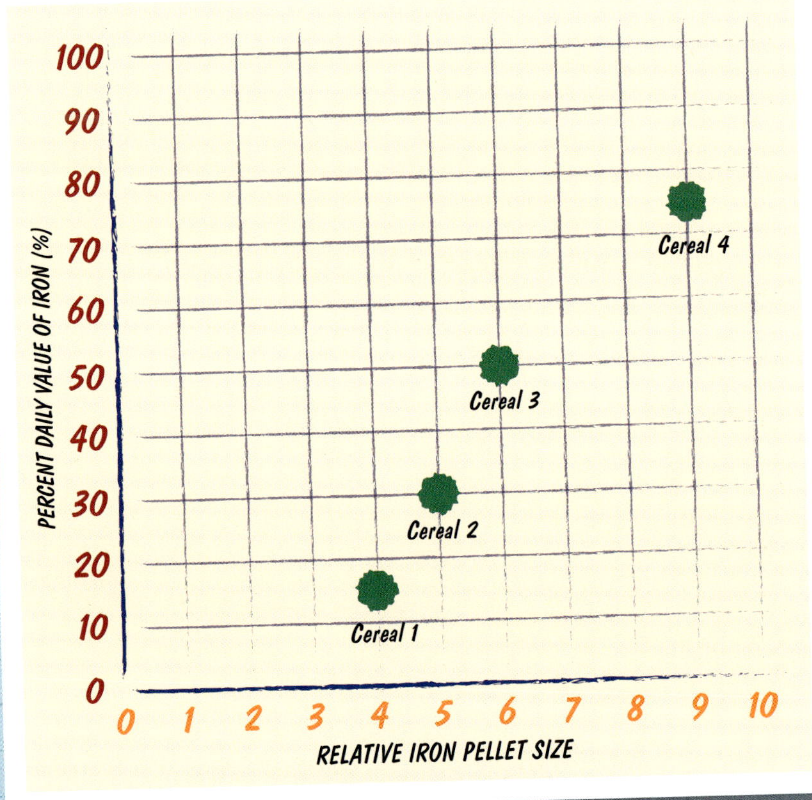

The Results Are In!

Now it is time to analyze your data and interpret your results. Write down everything that you learned from your investigation. For example, which cereal had the most iron and which had the least? Do your results match the Nutrition Facts labels? Evaluate all the information that you gathered and then communicate your findings to your family and friends. They will be bowled over by your cereal study!

THE FUTURE OF FOOD SCIENCE

Today, there are more than seven billion people on Earth. By the year 2050, the world's population is expected to grow to more than nine billion. A growing population means a greater demand for safe and nutritious food products. As the demand for food increases, so does the need for food scientists. The number of jobs in this field is increasing—and is expected to keep growing in the future.

A new grocery store in Milan, Italy—called the Supermarket of the Future—allows shoppers to find out exactly where food items came from and how they were produced.

If you would like a career in this important field, you will need to study hard in school. Food scientists are smart cookies! Most have bachelor's degrees in food science, chemistry, microbiology, or related subjects. Many continue their education to achieve advanced degrees. They often find work for food companies, universities, or governments.

From the Field: Mark Post

Mark Post has given the world a taste of things to come. The Dutch scientist recently grew the first beef hamburger in a lab. To make the burger, Post took cells from a cow and turned them into tiny strips of muscle. Then he combined the strips over time to form a burger patty. Now Post is investigating how to grow meat in large quantities for an affordable price. Growing meat in labs does not harm animals and could help combat world hunger.

Mark Post munches on the burger he grew in his science lab.

Get Involved!

If you're hungry for food science, you can do important investigations now! A 16-year-old student from South Africa recently did just that. Kiara Nirghin used waste products from the juice industry to develop a super-absorbent mixture. The mixture—made up of orange peels and avocado skins—can be applied to soil. When it rains, the mixture absorbs and holds large amounts of water, which crops can use to grow during periods with little or no rainfall.

Student Kiara Nirghin explains her juicy food science idea.

Big Data

You can also join the scientific community and get involved with citizen-science projects. Citizen-science is scientific research that is carried out by members of the public. People collect and analyze data and then submit their results to scientists who are conducting global investigations. The data that food scientists collect help them learn more about food and food processes all around the world. For example, there is a citizen-science project underway in which people measure the amount of vitamin C in their fruits and vegetables and then post the data on a website. In another project, people bake sourdough bread and submit pictures of it. Food scientists analyze the crumbs and air bubbles to learn about the **microbes** in the bread.

These students are getting a taste of food science! They are testing the ice cream that they made in a chemistry experiment.

LEARNING MORE

BOOKS

The Exploratorium. *Exploring Kitchen Science: 30+ Edible Experiments and Kitchen Activities.* Weldon Owen, 2015.

Katirgis, Jane. *STEM Jobs in Food and Nutrition.* Rourke Publishing Group, 2014.

Somervill, Barbara A. *Food Scientist.* Cherry Lake Publishing, 2014.

Ventura, Marne. *The 12 Biggest Breakthroughs in Food Technology.* 12-Story Library, 2015.

Wheeler-Toppen, Jodi, and Carol Tennant. *Edible Science: Experiments You Can Eat.* National Geographic Children's Books, 2015.

PLACES TO VISIT

Canada Agriculture and Food Museum
Ottawa, Ontario
Visit this Canadian museum for exhibitions on food safety, preservation, innovation, and other tasty topics. Or check out the online exhibition called "Food for Health" to learn about good bacteria, sodium, foodborne illness, and more.
https://foodforhealth.techno-science.ca

Smithsonian National Museum of American History
Washington, D.C.
Visit this American museum to learn about food automation and innovation, new materials and tools, snack engineering, and more at the exhibition called "Food: Transforming the American Table 1950–2000."
http://americanhistory.si.edu/food

ONLINE

www.sciencebuddies.org/science-engineering-careers/earth-physical-sciences/food-scientist-or-technologist
Visit this website for project ideas and key facts about food scientists.

www.ift.org/Knowledge-Center/Learn-About-Food-Science/Day-In-The-Life.aspx
Watch short videos to see the type of work that food scientists do each day.

www.sciencejournalforkids.org/science-articles/category/food-security
Read peer-reviewed science articles about food security and other important topics.

www.asc-csa.gc.ca/eng/astronauts/living-in-space/eating-in-space.asp
Learn more about food science in space and watch astronaut Chris Hadfield get cooking!

https://scistarter.com/finder
Browse this website for a citizen-science food project you can sink your teeth into.

GLOSSARY

acidity The quality of being an acid, a sour-tasting material that is the opposite of a base

artificial Made by people rather than occurring naturally

computational thinking A problem-solving process that involves breaking a problem into parts or steps, finding patterns, developing instructions to solve the problem, and forming rules or ideas from the patterns

consistency How firm or runny a substance is

consume To eat or drink something

contaminate To make food or other items dirty, impure, or dangerous by adding harmful substances to them

data Raw facts and figures collected from observations and measurements

digest To break down food into substances that can be absorbed and used by the body

distilled water Water that has been made pure by boiling it into steam and then condensing it back into liquid in a separate container

DNA A substance found in the cells of plants and animals that carries all the information about how they will look and function

emission A gas or other substance that is released into the air from cars, factories, and other sources

environmentally friendly Designed or used in a way that does not harm the environment

fiber A thin thread of material

formulate To create or invent something by careful thought and effort

gravity The natural force that pulls objects down toward Earth

International Space Station A large spacecraft that orbits Earth and on which astronauts live and conduct scientific research

microbe An extremely small living thing that can only be seen with a microscope

mineral A chemical substance, such as iron or zinc, that occurs naturally in some foods and that is important for good health

molecular Relating to a molecule, the smallest amount of a substance that has all the characteristics of that substance

nutrient A substance that living things get from food and that they need to grow and stay healthy

Nutrition Facts A label on packaged food that shows the amount of fat, sugar, protein, and other nutrients it contains

pH A number between 0 and 14 that shows if a chemical is an acid or a base

phenomena Facts or events that are of interest to scientists and can be described or explained scientifically

protein A substance found in meat, eggs, beans, and other foods that is an important part of the human diet

radiation Powerful rays of energy that can be dangerous

raw ingredient A substance, such as sugar, in its natural form; used to make food products

scientific journal A magazine that publishes important scientific discoveries

sensory Relating to the five senses of taste, smell, sight, hearing, and touch

shelf life How long foods can be stored before they go bad

survey An activity in which people are asked a series of questions to gather information

sustainable Able to produce food over time without harming the environment or using up limited natural resources

test kitchen A kitchen used to develop new kinds of foods

vitamin A natural substance that is usually found in foods and that helps your body to be healthy

yeast A single-celled fungus that is used to make alcoholic beverages and in baking to help make dough rise

INDEX

ABOUT THE AUTHOR

Robin Johnson is hungry for answers. Armed with an English degree, she has investigated weather, waves, animals, ecosystems, and many other science topics—and written more than 75 children's books. When she isn't using her noodle to put food on the table, Robin experiments in the kitchen with her engineer husband and two sons, and continues her global quest for the perfect cupcake.